Travel Journal

My trip to:

____

If lost please return to:

Name: _______________________

Phone: _______________________

Email: _______________________

Things to do before I go...

- [ ]
- [ ]
- [ ]
- [ ]
- [ ]
- [ ]
- [ ]
- [ ]
- [ ]
- [ ]
- [ ]
- [ ]
- [ ]
- [ ]
- [ ]
- [ ]
- [ ]
- [ ]

Flight, Hotels, Car Rental Info...

____

____

____

____

____

____

Packing List

____

____

____

____

____

____

____

____

____

One my trip I would like to...

____

____

____

____

____

____

____

Basic Foreign word/phrases...

____

____

____

____

____

____

Daily Travel Journal

Date/City/Weather

Places I am planning to visit Today

What to pack in my backpack

Best places I visited Today

My favorite local meal

My favorite part of the day

New words I learned Today

Notes/Funny memories/Anecdotes

Daily Travel Journal

Date/City/Weather

Places I am planning to visit Today

What to pack in my backpack

Best places I visited Today

My favorite local meal

My favorite part of the day

New words I learned Today

Notes/Funny memories/Anecdotes

Daily Travel Journal

Date/City/Weather

Places I am planning to visit Today

What to pack in my backpack

Best places I visited Today

My favorite local meal

My favorite part of the day

New words I learned Today

Notes/Funny memories/Anecdotes

Daily Travel Journal

Date/City/Weather

Places I am planning to visit Today

What to pack in my backpack

Best places I visited Today

My favorite local meal

My favorite part of the day

New words I learned Today

Notes/Funny memories/Anecdotes

Daily Travel Journal

Date/City/Weather

____

____

____

Places I am planning to visit Today

____

____

____

____

What to pack in my backpack

____

____

____

Best places I visited Today

____

____

____

My favorite local meal

____

____

____

____

My favorite part of the day

____

____

____

New words I learned Today

____

____

____

Notes/Funny memories/Anecdotes

____

____

____

____

____

____

____

____

____

 # Daily Travel Journal 

Date/City/Weather

____

____

____

Places I am planning to visit Today

____

____

____

____

What to pack in my backpack

____

____

____

Best places I visited Today

My favorite local meal

My favorite part of the day

New words I learned Today

Notes/Funny memories/Anecdotes

Daily Travel Journal

Date/City/Weather

Places I am planning to visit Today

What to pack in my backpack

Best places I visited Today

My favorite local meal

My favorite part of the day

New words I learned Today

Notes/Funny memories/Anecdotes

Daily Travel Journal

Date/City/Weather

Places I am planning to visit Today

What to pack in my backpack

Best places I visited Today

My favorite local meal

My favorite part of the day

New words I learned Today

Notes/Funny memories/Anecdotes

Daily Travel Journal

Date/City/Weather

Places I am planning to visit Today

What to pack in my backpack

Best places I visited Today

My favorite local meal

My favorite part of the day

New words I learned Today

Notes/Funny memories/Anecdotes

Daily Travel Journal

Date/City/Weather

Places I am planning to visit Today

What to pack in my backpack

Best places I visited Today

My favorite local meal

My favorite part of the day

New words I learned Today

Notes/Funny memories/Anecdotes

# Daily Travel Journal

Date/City/Weather

Places I am planning to visit Today

What to pack in my backpack

Best places I visited Today

My favorite local meal

My favorite part of the day

New words I learned Today

Notes/Funny memories/Anecdotes

Daily Travel Journal

Date/City/Weather

Places I am planning to visit Today

What to pack in my backpack

Best places I visited Today

My favorite local meal

My favorite part of the day

New words I learned Today

Notes/Funny memories/Anecdotes

Daily Travel Journal

Date/City/Weather

Places I am planning to visit Today

What to pack in my backpack

Best places I visited Today

My favorite local meal

My favorite part of the day

New words I learned Today

Notes/Funny memories/Anecdotes

 # Daily Travel Journal 

Date/City/Weather

___

___

___

Places I am planning to visit Today

___

___

___

___

What to pack in my backpack

___

___

___

Best places I visited Today

____

____

____

My favorite local meal

____

____

____

____

My favorite part of the day

____

____

____

New words I learned Today

Notes/Funny memories/Anecdotes

 # Daily Travel Journal 

Date/City/Weather

Places I am planning to visit Today

What to pack in my backpack

Best places I visited Today

My favorite local meal

My favorite part of the day

New words I learned Today

Notes/Funny memories/Anecdotes

 # Daily Travel Journal 

Date/City/Weather

Places I am planning to visit Today

What to pack in my backpack

Best places I visited Today

My favorite local meal

My favorite part of the day

New words I learned Today

Notes/Funny memories/Anecdotes

Daily Travel Journal

Date/City/Weather

Places I am planning to visit Today

What to pack in my backpack

Best places I visited Today

My favorite local meal

My favorite part of the day

New words I learned Today

Notes/Funny memories/Anecdotes

 # Daily Travel Journal 

Date/City/Weather

Places I am planning to visit Today

What to pack in my backpack

Best places I visited Today

My favorite local meal

My favorite part of the day

New words I learned Today

Notes/Funny memories/Anecdotes

Daily Travel Journal

Date/City/Weather

Places I am planning to visit Today

What to pack in my backpack

Best places I visited Today

My favorite local meal

My favorite part of the day

New words I learned Today

Notes/Funny memories/Anecdotes

Daily Travel Journal

Date/City/Weather

Places I am planning to visit Today

What to pack in my backpack

Best places I visited Today

____

____

____

My favorite local meal

____

____

____

____

My favorite part of the day

____

____

____

New words I learned Today

Notes/Funny memories/Anecdotes

Daily Travel Journal

Date/City/Weather

Places I am planning to visit Today

What to pack in my backpack

Best places I visited Today

My favorite local meal

My favorite part of the day

New words I learned Today

Notes/Funny memories/Anecdotes

 # Daily Travel Journal 

Date/City/Weather

Places I am planning to visit Today

What to pack in my backpack

Best places I visited Today

My favorite local meal

My favorite part of the day

New words I learned Today

____

____

____

Notes/Funny memories/Anecdotes

____

____

____

____

____

____

____

____

Daily Travel Journal

Date/City/Weather

Places I am planning to visit Today

What to pack in my backpack

Best places I visited Today

My favorite local meal

My favorite part of the day

New words I learned Today

Notes/Funny memories/Anecdotes

Daily Travel Journal

Date/City/Weather

Places I am planning to visit Today

What to pack in my backpack

Best places I visited Today

____

____

____

My favorite local meal

____

____

____

____

My favorite part of the day

____

____

____

New words I learned Today

Notes/Funny memories/Anecdotes

Daily Travel Journal

Date/City/Weather

Places I am planning to visit Today

What to pack in my backpack

Best places I visited Today

My favorite local meal

My favorite part of the day

New words I learned Today

Notes/Funny memories/Anecdotes

Daily Travel Journal

Date/City/Weather

____

____

____

Places I am planning to visit Today

____

____

____

____

What to pack in my backpack

____

____

____

____

Best places I visited Today

____

____

____

My favorite local meal

____

____

____

____

My favorite part of the day

____

____

____

New words I learned Today

Notes/Funny memories/Anecdotes

Daily Travel Journal

Date/City/Weather

Places I am planning to visit Today

What to pack in my backpack

Best places I visited Today

My favorite local meal

My favorite part of the day

New words I learned Today

Notes/Funny memories/Anecdotes

 # Daily Travel Journal 

Date/City/Weather

Places I am planning to visit Today

What to pack in my backpack

Best places I visited Today

My favorite local meal

My favorite part of the day

New words I learned Today

Notes/Funny memories/Anecdotes

 # Daily Travel Journal 

Date/City/Weather

Places I am planning to visit Today

What to pack in my backpack

Best places I visited Today

My favorite local meal

My favorite part of the day

New words I learned Today

Notes/Funny memories/Anecdotes

Daily Travel Journal

Date/City/Weather

Places I am planning to visit Today

What to pack in my backpack

Best places I visited Today

My favorite local meal

My favorite part of the day

New words I learned Today

Notes/Funny memories/Anecdotes

 # Daily Travel Journal 

Date/City/Weather

____

____

Places I am planning to visit Today

____

____

____

____

What to pack in my backpack

____

____

____

____

Best places I visited Today

My favorite local meal

My favorite part of the day

New words I learned Today

Notes/Funny memories/Anecdotes

Daily Travel Journal

Date/City/Weather

Places I am planning to visit Today

What to pack in my backpack

Best places I visited Today

My favorite local meal

My favorite part of the day

New words I learned Today

Notes/Funny memories/Anecdotes

Daily Travel Journal

Date/City/Weather

____

____

____

Places I am planning to visit Today

____

____

____

____

What to pack in my backpack

____

____

____

Best places I visited Today

My favorite local meal

My favorite part of the day

New words I learned Today

Notes/Funny memories/Anecdotes

 # Daily Travel Journal 

Date/City/Weather

Places I am planning to visit Today

What to pack in my backpack

Best places I visited Today

____

____

____

My favorite local meal

____

____

____

____

My favorite part of the day

____

____

____

New words I learned Today

Notes/Funny memories/Anecdotes

# Daily Travel Journal

Date/City/Weather

Places I am planning to visit Today

What to pack in my backpack

Date/City/Weather

Best places I visited Today

My favorite local meal

My favorite part of the day

New words I learned Today

Notes/Funny memories/Anecdotes

 # Daily Travel Journal 

Date/City/Weather

Places I am planning to visit Today

What to pack in my backpack

Best places I visited Today

____

____

____

My favorite local meal

____

____

____

____

My favorite part of the day

____

____

____

New words I learned Today

Notes/Funny memories/Anecdotes

Made in the USA
Monee, IL
07 July 2026

56686375R00069